The Catcher in the Rye

BookCaps Study Guide
www.bookcaps.com

Table of Contents:

Historical Context

J.D. Salinger wrote "The Catcher in the Rye" at a time when the world was expected to conform to the education and social norms of the time, no questions asked. Thus, his novel was not well-received by all because of the flagrant use of profanity, disregard for rules, disgust for conformity, and focus on sexual relationships.

Salinger, like Holden Caulfield, attended various prep schools and had an affinity for rule breaking. Holden seems to be the character that Salinger could live vicariously through. Holden hates everyone, especially those who were willing to conform to be exactly what they "should" be. He hates the world he belongs to and refuses to be what they want him to be because he is disgusted with a world that cares nothing about the individuals in it, but only its own prosperity.

Holden is extremely untrusting of adults and sees no merits in living in a "phony" adult society, which may reflect Salinger's experiences fighting in World War II. Holden Caulfield is a symbol of youth and innocence, something Salinger saw disappear rapidly in his experiences.

In a world that was just beginning to thrive, full of people happy to conform to its social norms, Salinger's only full-length novel became a source of controversy. In some areas of the country, "The Catcher in the Rye" is still banned from school reading lists and general education. The book is seen as inappropriate, rebellious, and offensive. In the parts of the country that do study this book, Holden Caulfield is seen as one of the most popular, complex, and interesting characters in literature.

Plot Overview

Holden Caulfield, the narrator of the story, is a sixteen-year-old boy living around the time of the 1950's in New York City. At the time he is telling the story he alludes to being in some sort of a mental hospital, obviously under treatment but goes on to tell his story.

Holden has been kicked out of three different prep schools and has just now been expelled from his fourth, Pencey prep, for failing all of his classes but one. At Pencey prep, Holden is surrounded by people who he finds annoying or disgusting in one way or another. He gets in a fight with his roommate, Stradlater, and decides to leave school early.

Once arriving in Manhattan, he decides to stay at the Edmont Hotel, rather than return home to his parents. Holden encounters many people whom he dislikes or finds disgusting in one way or another, tries to lose his virginity but cannot fathom why he would want to go through with such a pointless adult ritual, and ceaselessly interrogates an old classmate about his sexual conquests.

Holden tells his sister Phoebe, one of the most important people in his life, that he plans to run away and she wants to come with him, which he refuses. He watches Phoebe ride a carousel in the park and is so happy just watching her that he cannot bring himself to leave and instead returns home where he gets "sick" and decides to spare his audience the rest of the details on his mental state.

Themes

Self-preservation

Holden alienates himself from those around him as a means of protecting himself from things he does not understand and cannot change. Holden does not allow himself to ever really get close to anyone, though he obviously wants to.

He allows people to use them but is too disgusted by them to get anything in return. Holden cannot fathom growing up and living in an adult world when it all seems so ridiculous to him. Innocence and childhood protects Holden and that is where he wishes to stay.

Phoniness

This is Holden's concept of adulthood, which comes up multiple times. He believes that all things adult are phony: relationships, sex, careers, education, personalities, etc. Most of what Holden hates about the people he encounters is actions that make them seem more adult, or phony, to him.

Anytime someone says or does something that makes them seem more responsible he loses respect for them immediately. He also hates people who act like something that he is sure they are not, like Stradlater. He tells Sally Hayes that she is a "pain in the ass" when she tells him that they cannot run away together.

Innocence

Holden is in the midst of the ultimate struggle to hold onto his innocence when everyone around him is insisting that he grow up. Phoebe is the main symbol of innocence in this novel, though she is wiser in many ways than Holden. He loves her so much because she is the epitome of what he always wants to be, a carefree child, though she is not naïve.

The only time Holden is happy in the entire story is when he is watching Phoebe ride the carousel, most likely because he is living vicariously through her, wishing that life could be that simple for him, once again.

Mortality

In the sense of this novel, mortality represents the death of childhood and innocence. This can be seen in the literal death of Holden's younger brother, Allie, much before his time, or in the death of childhood in the face of adulthood.

Holden seems to be terrified of both options, which is obvious in the way he misses Allie, as well as his quest for irresponsibility and rebellion. To Holden, it seems, the death of his innocence is the death of his soul. Holden hints to the fact that he may have been molested as a child, and Jane may have been as well. This could be the death of youth for Holden, though he is in denial about its effects.

Youth

The happiest time that Holden has in his memory involve things that happened in his youth, or people he views as youthful and carefree. The only people Holden really admires or truly cares about are his brother Allie, who died as a child, his little sister Phoebe who despite her wisdom is still an innocent, and Jane Gallagher, with whom he had a very solid friendship/relationship with in his younger years. Youth is the equivalent to happiness for Holden, and it is his fear that once he reaches adulthood and leaves childhood behind, he may never be truly happy again.

Isolation

Holden is isolated and lonely as he states many times throughout his story, but by his own hand. He makes an attempt to befriend people, by letting them borrow things, or paying their tabs, but says nothing to them about it, he simply complains to himself.

He knows he is being used but he cannot stop himself from wanting others to be happy, even through his own misery, nor can he stop himself from being disgusting with certain characteristics of others. Holden is isolated because while he wishes he were not lonely, he cannot bring himself to truly care about anyone other than a select few.

Sexuality

Holden seems to be obsessed with sex, and anyone who has had it, but does not understand the need for it in his life. He wants to know if Stradlater tried to have sex with Jane, but more so to know if Jane has taken that step toward adulthood then because he is jealous.

Holden also questions Carl Luce of his sexual exploitations, mostly because he is trying to understand what makes people want to have sex. He tries, half-heartedly, one night to lose his virginity, going so far as to hire a prostitute, but just cannot bring himself to do it. He feels that sex is something adults do and it has no meaning at all. Molestation could be the reason that Holden feels no good can come from sex.

Depression

Everything Holden encounters is something he finds to be depressing. He thinks that people who try to be something they are not are depressing, that adult sexual relationships are depressing, that school and finding a career is depressing, and that normal human relationships are depressing. It feels obvious that what Holden actually finds depressing is the idea of growing up, and perhaps fears of the unknown. Holden allows his surroundings to depress him because he does not wish to deal with the changes that lie ahead of him. He is depressed by the idea of leaving behind everything he knows, and with the possibility of losing those few whom he cares about, for a future that he is not prepared for.

Knowledge vs. Wisdom

Holden draws a fine, yet definite, line between conventional knowledge and wisdom. Many people he encounters, mostly at school, he finds to be extremely dumb. The fact that they attend prep school and seem to make use of their time there, unlike Holden, alludes to the fact that they are, in fact, book smart; however, in terms of life Holden finds them to be quite stupid.

He thinks that his younger siblings, Allie and Phoebe, are two of the wisest people he has ever met and they are nothing but children. Conventional smarts hold no bearing with Holden; it is wisdom that he admires.

Religion

Holden feels the same way about religion as he does about everything that has been institutionalized: it has merit on its own, but has been ruined by society and authority. Religion is something that one person, of his or her own free will, can research and figure out for himself and it will have a very significant and different meaning to each who finds it. However, when that religion is taught in a group setting it becomes almost cult-like and something that no longer holds any merit because it is being taught, rather than discovered. This is how Holden feels about conformity in all areas of life, with religion merely acting as an example.

Characters

Holden Caulfield

The narrator and protagonist of the story, Holden tells the story from, presumably, an institution where he is receiving mental help. Holden is a sixteen-year-old boy who is stuck between childhood and adulthood, with disgust for conformity in all areas of life. He dislikes nearly everyone he meets yet feels extremely lonely.

He makes an attempt to get close to people but does not seem to go about it, other than letting people walk all over him. He is disgusted with the world he is living in and the hypocrisy of it all. Holden often displays some of the characteristics that he hates in others, while on his road to discovery but never seems to realize it for himself. The only people he respects in life are those who are children, whom he finds much wiser than adults.

Phoebe Caulfield

Holden's younger sister and the most important female in his life, Phoebe represents everything that Holden values in life: youth, innocence, freedom, and wisdom. Holden considers Phoebe to be one of the wisest people he knows, despite her lesser years on Earth and he turns to her when he needs advice.

Phoebe is the reason Holden does not run away, because he cannot risk losing one of the few people whom he holds so close. Phoebe is one of the few people who actually understand Holden and the fact that the only person he is harming in his disdain is himself.

Allie Caulfield

Allie was Holden's younger brother who died of Leukemia a few years prior to the start of Holden's story. Allie is a sterling example of exactly what Holden fears: the loss of innocence. Allie's innocence was stolen from him tragically, and Holden feels that conformity is just another way of blatantly stealing one's youth and freewill.

Allie was very important to Holden and his death hit Holden hard. Holden carries around with him Allie's old baseball glove, which is covered with poems that Allie used to write. The baseball glove is the single most important possession to Holden.

D.B. Caulfield

D.B. is Holden's other brother, whom he does not have as much respect for as he does for Allie and Phoebe. D.B. had once written a volume of short stories, which Holden loves and carries around with him always, but Holden feels as though D.B. sold out in his career as a Hollywood writer.

Holden often credits D.B. as being his very favorite writer, though he does not respect his career choice. D.B. has done what Holden hates the most; he has conformed to the social norms and expectations that Holden avoids at all costs. Holden does not find D.B.to be as wise as his other, younger, siblings and does not seem to hold him in as high regard as he does Phoebe and Allie.

Ackley

Ackley is a classmate of Holden's at Pencey Prep. He lives down the hall from Holden and Holden is disgusted by Ackley's obvious lack of personal hygiene. Ackley is a nerdy guy with a bad acne problem and terrible dental habits.

Ackley constantly tries to be friends with Holden, though it is obvious that Holden has no desire to be friends with him, or even to be around him most of the time. Holden hates people who lie for the sake of lying and believes that Ackley makes up stories about his life to make him appear cooler to his classmates.

Stradlater

Stradlater is Holden's roommate at Pencey Prep and has a similar disdain for Ackley and his hygiene problems. Holden does not appear to hate Stradlater the same way he hates others, though he does find his appearance, and general personality, to be rather annoying. Stradlater takes Jane Gallagher on a date, which bothers Holden slightly.

When Holden asks Stradlater if he tried to make Jane Gallagher have sex with him, Stradlater messes with Holden to get a rise out of him and Holden attacks him. Stradlater is good looking, popular, and sexually active, though Holden points out that he is quite the slob and rather disgusting.

Jane Gallagher

Jane is the only female that is not related to Holden whom he actually has feelings for. He finds Jane attractive, and also respects her, which is a combination that happens rarely for Holden. Holden and Jane were very close one summer when their families vacationed next to one another and this summer is one of the best memories Holden has in his life, thus he reflects on his time with Jane often. Jane does not actually appear in the story, but is mentioned quite a few times and obviously means a lot to Holden.

Sally Hayes

Sally has been Holden's on/off girlfriend for quite some time. While Holden does seem to like Sally more than he likes most people, he is still annoyed by her a lot of the time. Holden believes that Sally is "dumb" and he dislikes how responsible she is when he wishes to be spontaneous.

He feels that Sally is extremely shallow but puts up with her so he has someone to make out with and spend a day with. Sally bores Holden at times but he is so lonely that he feels he needs to spend time with her.

Mr. Antolini

Mr. Antolini was Holden's English teacher at Elkton Hills School and is good friends with Holden's parents. He is married to a much older and very unattractive woman who is very wealthy. Mr. Antolini is almost definitely gay, with his wife acting as a cover-up, and Holden believes that Mr. Antolini comes on to him one night when he stays at his house out of despair.

He calls Holden "handsome" and watches him sleep while brushing his hair off his forehead. Holden is very uncomfortable with this and leaves the house immediately. Holden hints at the fact that he has been molested in the past that makes this situation especially uncomfortable.

Mr. Spencer

Holden's history teacher at Pencey, Mr. Spencer epitomizes everything Holden finds boring about becoming an adult. He is old, unremarkable, goes to the same boring job every single day, plays tennis, and has martinis with the same boring group of friends.

Mr. Spencer understands Holden to a point and is determined to fix Holden's academic problems and help him to make something of his life. Holden, of course, is not on the same page as Mr. Spencer and has no desire to conform to that life.

Carl Luce

A student at Columbia whom Holden knows from his time as the Whooten School where Carl acted as Holden's student advisor. Holden does not particularly like Carl but invites him out for drinks regardless. Holden knows that Carl has quite a bit of sexual experience so he interrogates him about his sexual escapades in an attempt to understand adult sexual relationships. Holden has a hard time finding purpose to sex and hopes that Carl can explain it to him.

The Two Nuns

The nuns are not actually characters, as much as a means for Holden to go off on a very informative tangent. Holden observes the nuns and rather than making the normal observations on appearance or superficial assumptions, Holden sees them as people and reads into their actions.

Holden digresses to a discussion about money and religion and the barriers that exist between people who come from different walks of life not being able to easily merge with one another. Holden makes it known that he understands people on a level that many others never even try to reach.

Maurice

Maurice is the elevator operator at the Edmont Hotel where Holden is staying when he first gets back to the city. Maurice offers to get Holden a prostitute, an offer that Holden takes him up on. While Holden pays the $5 even though he does not have sex with her, Maurice demands an extra $5 for not following through. When Holden refuses Maurice punches him in the stomach and steals the $5 from him.

Sunny

The prostitute that Maurice sends up to Holden's room. Sunny is a young girl, about Holden's age and when Holden sees her and her innocent appearance he cannot fathom having sex with her. He does not understand how people can be so excited about sex when he just finds it dirty and disturbing.

Holden's compassion forces him to see Sunny as a real person, rather than a hooker. He pays her anyway but she is not satisfied and tries to get him to change his mind. When Holden still refuses she gets Maurice to come and demand more money for her troubles.

Mrs. Morrow

The mother of one of Holden's classmates at Pencey, Ernest Morrow, whom Holden runs into on the train from Pencey back to Manhattan. Holden tells Mrs. Morrow that his name is Rudolph Schmidt, who is actually a janitor at the school, and makes up ridiculous stories about himself for no reason at all. Holden does not particularly like Ernest yet tells his mother that he is a real popular kid and has a ton of friends and is a great student. Holden feels that since Mrs. Morrow thinks so highly of her son, he will not give her reason to feel any differently.

Chapter 1

We are introduced to the narrator and protagonist, Holden Caulfield, a sixteen-year-old boy who confined to an institution for mental health, where he is being treated. Holden does not wish to reveal anything about his younger years, merely touching on the subject of his siblings.

He mentions his older brother, D.B., who is a fantastic writer, but sold out for a career of writing in Hollywood, rather than writing substantial literature. Holden is disappointed in D.B.'s career choice and wishes he had become a respectable author instead. Holden attends Pencey Prep, a well-known prep school in Pennsylvania. Holden is being expelled from Pencey because he is failing every class, except English, and he tries to think of a creative way to leave the school.

He is watching the annual football game, thinking of how he lost the fencing team's equipment when they were on their way to a meet when he was the one in charge of it. He decides that he is going to say goodbye to his history teacher, Mr. Spencer, and so he decides to run to Mr. Spencer's house, taking a break along the way because he smokes too much.

Chapter 2

Holden appears to be quite close to both Mr. Spencer and his wife and it becomes obvious that Mr. Spencer feels a bond with Holden. Mr. Spencer is very sick with the flu and Holden seems to be rather disgusted by his position yet stays to speak with him anyway. Knowing that Holden has just flunked out of Pencey, he being one of the teachers who failed him, Mr. Spencer attempts to speak to Holden about his education and the importance of taking it seriously. It becomes apparent that Holden holds his education in no high regard and does not wish to listen to this lecture.

Mr. Spencer tells Holden that he must learn to play by the rules in the game of life if he wishes to get somewhere with it. He reads Holden the dismal final essay that he wrote, trying to get the point across that he is not even making an effort to pass his classes. After one final attempt to get Holden to think of his future and see the value in finishing school and putting some real effort into it, he is interrupted by Holden who says goodbye and leaves him.

Chapter 3

After leaving Mr. Spencer's home Holden returns to Ossenburger Hall, his dorm at Pencey. The dormitory is named after a Pencey alumnus who made his money selling discount funeral equipment, which Holden mentions in the way that it is obvious he is unimpressed.

Holden puts on his new hunting hat and reads "Out of Africa" by Isak Dinesen. While he is reading, he is interrupted by Ackley, a boy who lives down the hall. Ackley feels as though he can just barge into Holden's room at any time and hang out with him, though Holden cannot stand him.

Holden makes it a point to mention that Ackley has a bad acne problem, even worse dental hygiene, and an overall lack of personal hygiene. He asks Holden a barrage of questions that do not matter, annoying Holden to no end and clips his fingernails all over Holden's floor which just about brings him to his breaking point.

Ackley has no friends but feels like everyone likes him and is considered lucky to know him, though he is obviously very irritating. Ackley finally leaves Holden alone when Stradlater, Holden's roommate, comes in because Ackley does not like him.

Chapter 4

Stradlater is Holden's very good-looking roommate who is also very popular and one of the few students at Pencey who is somewhat sexually experienced. Stradlater tells Holden that he has a big date later and he wants to shave before he leaves.

Holden decides to go to the bathroom with Stradlater while he shaves just for something to do. Holden notices that while Stradlater is much better looking than Ackley and much less annoying, he is almost equally as disgusting. Ackley is outwardly gross but Stradlater is a "secret slob" because he does not keep his toiletries clean. Stradlater asks Holden to do his English essay for him because he will not have time to do it himself with his date.

Holden discovers that Stradlater's date is a girl named Jane Gallagher whom Holden was very close with one summer and obviously has very strong feelings for still. Holden is very annoyed when Stradlater calls her "Jean" and Holden feels the need to tell him insignificant details about Jane that only someone who really cared about her would notice, such as the fact that when she plays checkers, she leaves all her kings in the back row. Holden loans Stradlater his jacket and decides not to say hello to Jane before the date.

Chapter 5

Holden has an underwhelming dinner in the dining hall then decides to go to a movie with his friend, Mal Broussard, and invites Ackley to go as well. The other two boys had already seen the movie so they decided to grab some burgers and play video games instead.

Once back at school, Mal goes off to find something to do, Holden decides to work on Stradlater's English assignment, and Ackley sits on Holden's bed popping his pimples, which Holden finds repulsive. Holden cannot think of anything to write Stradlater's paper on so he decides to write about his kid brother Allie's baseball mitt, which he would write his poems in. Allie died of Leukemia several years before the start of the novel and it is obvious that Holden misses him very much. He admires Allie's intelligence and innocence. Though Allie was younger than him, Holden states that he was the most intelligent person in the Caulfield family.

The night he found out that Allie had died he sat in the garage at his home and punched out all of the windows with his bare hands. After Ackley leaves, Holden reflects on Allie and how he misses him, while staring out the window.

Chapter 6

Stradlater comes home from his date with Jane and reads the essay that Holden has written for him. He realizes that Holden has written about Allie's mitt, which has nothing at all to do with the assignment and he gets upset with him.

Holden is offended that Stradlater insults the essay so he gets angry at him and rips it up. Holden asks Stradlater questions about his date, mainly to find out if he tried to have sex with Jane, and Stradlater will not give him any straight answers. Holden seems extremely upset at the idea of Jane having sex, but not necessarily due to jealousy.

Holden grows increasingly frustrated with Stradlater's avoidance so he attacks him. Being much bigger and stronger, Stradlater pins Holden down, hoping to calm him but Holden keeps egging Stradlater on until he punches Holden in the face, causing his nose to bleed. Stradlater is worried that he has really hurt Holden and thus will be in trouble and Holden finds his worrying ridiculous.

Holden keeps taunting Stradlater, eventually causing Stradlater to leave the room. Holden then goes to visit Ackley, nose still bloodied.

Chapter 7

Holden spends some time talking with Ackley, obviously troubled. Ackley's roommate is not around so Holden decides to try to sleep in his bed, as to avoid going back to his own room and seeing Stradlater again. Holden cannot fall asleep and begins wondering what he can do with his life after leaving Pencey.

He wonders aloud if he can become a monk without being a Catholic and Ackley starts to get annoyed with him. Holden, deciding that Ackley is "phony", gets annoyed right back and decides that rather than wait until Wednesday, when he was originally meant to leave Pencey, he would leave that night and hide out for three days in the city before returning to his parents apartment.

Holden knows that his parents will be very upset that he is being expelled from yet another school so he wishes to give them a couple of days to mull things over before he sees them. Holden returns to his room to pack his belongs, puts on his hunting hat and leaves Pencey forever, loudly calling all of the boys in his dorm "morons" before vacating.

Chapter 8

Holden gets on a train to go back to New York City where he meets a middle-aged woman who is very attractive. He learns that this woman is Mrs. Morrow, the mother of Ernest Morrow, one of Holden's classmates at Pencey.

Holden introduces himself as Rudolph Schmidt, which is actually the name of the janitor in the dormitory Holden lived in. He tells Mrs. Morrow that he has a brain tumor and is headed to the city to have it operated on, though this is not true in the least. Though he is not a fan of Ernest, Holden tells Mrs. Morrow wonderful things about him because it is obvious that she is very proud of him and wishes to know he is doing well. Holden tells her that Ernest should have been elected class president, if only he would have let his classmates nominate him.

Also, he tells her that Ernest is the most popular boy at the school, though that is not the truth, and she seems very happy to hear this news. Holden seems to want to make people happy, even if he has to tell lies to do so.

Chapter 9

Holden arrives in Penn Station and wishes to call someone, though he cannot decide who to call. He seems to make up an excuse to not call each person that he thinks of. He considers calling his little sister, Phoebe, but knows that she will be asleep and does not wish to wake her. He thinks of calling his brother D.B., and then remembers that D.B. is in Hollywood. He thinks of Jane Gallagher but decides against it, possibly because he is still bitter about her date with Stradlater and he almost calls Sally Hayes, a girl he has been seeing, but does not want to talk to her mother, knowing that her mother dislikes him. Holden gives up on the idea of calling anyone and instead decides to check into the Edmont Hotel. Once he checks into the Edmont he looks out the window and sees a man dressing up in women's clothing and a couple spitting drinks in one another's faces. Holden decides that he wants to have sex now, and calls a girl who someone told him would sleep with him but when she tells him that he will have to wait until tomorrow he gets aggravated and hangs up on her.

Chapter 10

Holden decides to leave his room and visit the hotel bar, calling the Lavender Room, in hope to get a drink. He briefly toys with the idea of calling Phoebe yet again, though knows it is far too late to call. He "introduces" us to Phoebe and has very similar things to say about her as he did about Allie. He feels that Phoebe is old for her age and extremely intelligent, with a talent for writing. He says that Phoebe's only downfall is the fact that she tends to be overly emotional.

Once at the Lavender Room, Holden attempts to buy a drink, believing that his height and graying hair will lead people to think he is older, but is denied. He begins talking to and dancing with three girls, one of whom he believes he is "in love" with because he is such a good dancer.

They tolerate him for a while but they quickly get bored with him and begin to laugh at him for trying to be so debonair. Holden is "depressed" by the fact that they care so much about celebrities and decides to leave, first paying the girls' bar tab.

Chapter 11

Holden leaves the bar and begins to think about Jane and the times they shared together in the past. Holden met Jane when their families were vacationing next to each other in Maine and quickly became friends. He remembers when they would play checkers together and how holding hands with her is something that made him truly happy.

One day when they were playing checkers, Holden recalls Jane's stepfather coming outside and asking her for cigarettes, Jane refusing. As soon as her stepfather returned to the house Jane started crying and Holden did not understand what was wrong and just started kissing her face all over.

Holden recalls that this was the closest they ever came to "necking" and says that their physical relationship never went much further than this, but they often held hands, which was enough for him. It is obvious that he cares greatly for Jane in the way he speaks of her.

Once Holden returns to his room he sees that all of the people he was watching through the windows earlier appear to have gone to bed and he decides that he is not yet ready to turn in and leaves the hotel once again.

Chapter 12

Holden decides to visit a bar called Ernie's that he and D.B. used to go to. Holden takes a liking to his cab driver, Horwitz, and for the second time in the same night he asks the cabbie where the ducks in the Central Park lagoon go during the winter. Unlike the first driver, who just ignored him, Horwitz gets very angry with Holden. Once Holden arrives at Ernie's he drinks a scotch and soda and settles in to listen to Ernie play piano, though Holden is unimpressed with his playing. Holden finds himself getting increasingly annoyed by the conversations happening around him. He finds nearly everyone to be phony and the phoniness of the people surrounding him is depressing to him.

Holden runs into Lillian Simmons, a girl who used to date his brother, D.B. Lillian is extremely annoying to Holden and he has a hard time having a conversation with her. In order to get away from Lillian, Holden decides that his only option is to leave Ernie's and so he does.

Chapter 13

As Holden is leaving Ernie's he is feeling quite cowardly for leaving to avoid Lillian rather than just telling her he does not wish to speak to her. This revelation leads to Holden realizing that he is, in fact, a coward and avoids confrontation at all costs, despite his fight with Stradlater.

Holden goes off on a tangent, thinking about his gloves that were stolen while he was at Pencey and imagines confronting the person who stole them, knowing full well that he would make no such confrontation.

Holden arrives at the hotel and gets in the elevator he meets Maurice, the elevator attendant, who offers to send him up a prostitute for five dollars. Holden is flustered and accepts the offer, feeling as though the fact that he is a coward is the reason he has never had sex with a woman.

When the prostitute, Sunny, arrives Holden becomes very uncomfortable at her youthful innocence, and increasingly more uncomfortable when she takes off her dress. Holden tells her that he cannot have sex with her because he is recovering from surgery, pays her the money anyway, and asks her to leave. Sunny tells him it is ten dollars, which Holden refuses, and she leaves very upset.

Chapter 14

After Sunny leaves, Holden sits alone in his room and smokes a few cigarettes, reminiscing about Allie. He recalls leaving Allie out of a game he was playing shortly before he died and instantly feels remorseful for it, even though it happened so long ago.

Holden considers praying but decides against it due to his disdain for organized religion, and tries to go to sleep when there is a knock at his door. Holden finds Maurice at the door, along with Sunny, demanding the extra five dollars from him. Holden refuses so Maurice pins him against the wall while Sunny steals the money from Holden's wallet.

Holden runs his mouth to Maurice, insulting him and thus Maurice punches Holden in the stomach and leaves him crumpled on the floor. Once Maurice leaves, Holden imagines getting revenge on Maurice like a mafia gangster, knowing that he would never confront someone in that way no matter how appealing the idea is. Holden eventually gives up on this idea, gets back into bed, and goes to sleep.

Chapter 15

When Holden awakes the next day he decides to give his sometimes-girlfriend, Sally Hayes, a call to make a date. Sally agrees to spend the day with Holden so he packs his things and checks out of the hotel. Holden goes to Grand Central Station to put his bags in a locker and wonders what would happen if he lost his things, noting that his father would be upset. This is the first time Holden mentions his parents in any detail. Holden seems to care for his mother quite a bit more than any other adult in his life. He states that his mother has not been quite the same since Allie passed away and hopes that his expulsion will not make her more ill.

Holden takes himself out to breakfast where he encounters two nuns and discusses "Romeo and Juliet" with them. In his mind, Holden digresses to a discussion about money and religion and the barriers it sets between different social classes. He muses that barriers make it difficult for people from different walks to become close to one another.

It becomes clear that Holden understands people on a deep level that even he is not aware of. He donates ten dollars to the nuns, though he does not believe in organized religion and later feels bad that he did not give them more.

Chapter 16

As Holden leaves the diner, he muses about how
generous the nuns are and totally selfless and believes
that he does not know anyone in his real life who is
like that. He seems to have great respect for the nuns,
beyond what he has for most other people.

Holden goes to a record store where he buys an album
for Phoebe that is sung by a black blues singer who
makes the innocent children's album sound raunchy.
He thinks about Phoebe and how although she is very
young she is very intelligent and is the only person
who really understands Holden and the things he says
and does.

Holden calls Jane but hangs up when her mother
answers, buys tickets for the show he and Sally will
see that night, and heads to the park to see if Phoebe
is there roller-skating as she sometimes does on
Sundays.

Holden cannot find Phoebe and walks to the Museum
of Natural History musing about how life there is
frozen forever and every time he visits he feels as
though he has changed so much and the exhibits are
always the same.

Chapter 17

Holden meets Sally at the Biltmore Hotel for their date. Holden and Sally make out in the cab on the way to the theater, which is one of the reasons that Holden likes to spend time with Sally. During the play, Holden is annoyed by the actors because he finds them too good, to the point that they are boring and obviously full of themselves.

Sally sees a boy that she knows from Andover, another prep school, during intermission and Holden sees her talking to him, assuming she is flirting, quickly become annoyed. Though he is upset with her he decides to take her ice-skating anyway, telling her she only wants to go so people can see how cute her butt looks in her short skirt.

Holden and Sally sit down to talk and Holden begins to quickly unravel, getting loud and belligerent at times. He complains about all of the people he finds phony and depressing and tells Sally they should run away together to live in a cabin away from the world. Sally tells him he is ridiculous, he calls her a "pain in the ass", and she begins to cry. Holden decides that he needs to go and leaves her there.

Chapter 18

Once Holden leaves Sally at the skating rink he gets himself a sandwich and again considers calling Jane. He remembers a time when Jane attended a dance with a guy that Holden found to be very arrogant but who Jane said had an inferiority complex.

Holden decided that is just what girls say to make an excuse for dating guys like him. Holden then decides to call Carl Luce. Carl was Holden's student advisor at Whooten School and is now a student at Columbia. Carl agrees to meet Holden at Wicker Bar later for some drinks. To kill some time, Holden goes to see a show at Radio City. He watches the Rockettes, which he deems superficial, but reminisces on some fond memories of Allie, then watches a war movie which he finds extremely boring.

After the movie, Holden heads to Wicker Bar to meet Carl, on his way considering the war movie he has just watched. Holden remembers a conversation he had with D.B. about being in the military and decides that he could never join the army.

Chapter 19

While waiting for Carl Luce at the Wicker Bar, Holden thinks about Luce and how they know one another. Carl is three years older than Holden, was once his student advisor at Whooten School, and is now a student at Columbia. While at Whooten, Luce would tell the other guys about his sexual exploits. Holden thinks that Carl is slightly feminine and phony, just like everyone else, but is amused by him regardless. When Carl arrives he does not seem happy to see Holden at all. Holden immediately begins asking Carl questions about sex, becoming increasingly confused about why adults feel the need to have sex at all when he feels uncomfortable when confronted with it face to face.

Carl refuses to get into the kind of discussions the boys used to have when at Whooten and tells Holden that he thinks he needs to be psychoanalyzed. Holden knows that Luce's father is a psychoanalyst and asks Carl if his father has ever psychoanalyzed him. Luce grows tired of Holden's obvious issues and annoying, immature behavior and leaves the bar.

Chapter 20

Holden is left alone at the bar by Luce and decides to keep drinking until he eventually gets very drunk. He unsuccessfully tries to speak to and get a date with two different women there: a lounge singer named Valencia, and the hat-check girl.

After being turned down by both women, Holden incoherently calls Sally Hayes, upsetting both her and her grandmother due to his drunkenness and the late hour of the phone call. Holden splashes some water over his head in an attempt to sober up and decides to see if the ducks are still at the lagoon in the park.

On his way to visit the ducks, Holden breaks the record he bought for Phoebe and is very upset about it. He then realizes that his hair is frozen from it being wet and wonders what would happy if he died of pneumonia. He says that he missed Allie's funeral because he was in the hospital from punching out the windows of the garage, though he later visited Allie's grave. He is disgusted with the idea of flowers being put on graves and decides that he needs to risk going home because he needs to speak with Phoebe.

Chapter 21

Holden arrives at his apartment building and is glad that he does not recognize the elevator operator who is on duty because he can lie to the substitute and pretend he is visiting the people who live across the hall from his parents.

Once Holden gets into the apartment he cannot find Phoebe in her room so he checks D.B.'s room because he knows that Phoebe likes to sleep in there sometimes when D.B. is not there. He reads through Phoebe's school books and is brought instant happiness and amusement by the notes she jots and the way she signs her name. He wakes Phoebe and she is ecstatic to see him and begins telling him about everything that has happened since the last time she spoke to him: D.B.'s new movie, a movie she recently saw, her school play, and a boy at school who she is bullied by, but she quickly realizes that Holden is home early and he must have gotten kicked out of yet another school.

Phoebe tells Holden, repeatedly, that their father is going to "kill" him and Holden tries to talk to her about it but she just covers her head with her pillow, refusing to listen. Holden leaves to go get cigarettes.

Chapter 22

When Holden returns from getting cigarettes he talks with Phoebe about why he has been kicked out of school again. He attempts to explain to her about the people he goes to school with, the teachers, and the classes and tells her he hates them all.

Phoebe, one of the few people who understand Holden, probably more so than he does, points out that Holden hates everything. When she asks him to think of one thing he does not hate all he thinks of are the nuns and this boy (James Castle) he went to school with in the past who jumped to his death after being bullied. He tells her that he does not hate Allie and Phoebe tells Holden that Allie is dead and does not count.

Phoebe asks Holden what he wants to do with his life and he misquotes a Robert Burns poem ("If a body catch a body, comin' through the rye") stating that he wants to be the person who catches the kids who are about to fall off the cliff when they are playing in the rye. Phoebe tells him he misquoted and it is, in fact, "If a body meet a body, comin' through the rye", thus his plan is foiled.

Chapter 23

Holden leaves Phoebe momentarily to call Mr.
Antolini, a man who was his English teacher when he
attended Elkton Hills, and a good friend of his
parents. Holden remembers how Mr. Antolini was
the only person who seemed to care when James
Castle jumped out that window, because he is a very
sympathetic and kind person.

Mr. Antolini is extremely upset when Holden informs
him that he has been kicked out of yet another school
and invites Holden to his house and offers to allow
him to spend the night. Holden goes back to
Phoebe's room and asks her to dance with him, which
she gladly agrees to.

After dancing together through a few songs Holden
hears his parents come through the front door.
Holden hides in Phoebe's closet until his parents have
gone to bed and decides to depart to Mr. Antolini's
house.

Before he leaves he tells Phoebe of his plan to move
out west all alone and leave his life in New York City
behind. Phoebe gives Holden all of her Christmas
money she had saved to help him on his way and as
he is leaving he gives Phoebe his red hunting hat.

Chapter 24

Holden arrives at Mr. Antolini's apartment and sees that he and his wife were just about to clean up from a dinner party they had and they obviously had been doing a bit of drinking. Mrs. Antolini brings them some coffee and Holden tries to explain to Mr. Antolini why he hates school so much. He tells Mr. Antolini that his debate team frowns upon digressions but Holden finds digressions to be interesting.

Mr. Antolini tries to explain to Holden that sticking to a subject can be just as interesting, in an attempt to make him realize that there are multiple ways of seeing every situation. Mr. Antolini tells Holden that he fears he is setting himself up for the kind of fall that leads to total isolation and hatred for the world in general. Holden does not seem to think things are that serious but Mr. Antolini wants him to think it through.

Mr. Antolini tries to make Holden see that if he stays in school he may learn a lot about himself and why he is the way he is. Holden seems to disagree and decides it is time to go to sleep. Holden awakes in the middle of the night to Mr. Antolini stroking his hair. Mr. Antolini could just be showing a sign of caring about Holden, much as his own child, but Holden takes it as a homosexual gesture and leaves immediately.

Chapter 25

Holden spends the night on a bench at Grand Central and wakes up feeling very overwhelmed with life. He feels as though he may literally disappear and talks, out loud, to his dead brother Allie as he walks around. He imagines living life as a hermit and being married to a deaf-mute that will never annoy him or be able to judge him. He decides to go to Phoebe's school and sends her a note to meet him at the Museum of Art so he can return the money she lent him.

While walking through the school, and again at the museum, he sees the words "fuck you" scrawled on walls. This depresses Holden and he wonders if when he dies it will say "fuck you" on his tombstone. Holden faints in the museum and plays it off like nothing happened.

Phoebe shows up to meet him with her bags packed and he tells her she cannot come with him and she gets mad at him and returns his hat and he feels as though he may pass out again. Holden convinces Phoebe to go to the zoo with him but she is still upset. Eventually Holden gives her back his hat and she is slightly less mad. As Phoebe rides the carousel in the park and Holden watches her he is the happiest he can ever remember being, to the point that it is overwhelming.

Chapter 26

Holden is done telling his story, and does not continue it from the day he was in the park with Phoebe. He simply states that after that day he got "sick" and was put in the rest home where he is telling his story from.

It is assumed that he is in a mental hospital, after nearly having a mental breakdown that last day with Phoebe. Holden immediately regrets telling his story to anyone, even D.B. who is one of the people who visits Holden fairly regularly.

Holden intends to begin going to a new school the following year, where he believes he may actually apply himself. Holden feels lonelier than ever because telling his story made him miss the people in it, though he was never actually close to any of them, other than Phoebe.

About BookCaps

We all need refreshers every now and then. Whether you are a student trying to cram for that big final, or someone just trying to understand a book more, BookCaps can help. We are a small, but growing company, and are adding titles every month. Visit www.bookcaps.com to see more of our books. Or contact us with any questions.

Made in the USA
Lexington, KY
10 September 2013